Bible Sticker and Activity Book

Moses in the Bulrushes

p

SLAVES IN EGYPT

The Israelites had lived happily in the land of Egypt for many, many years. But the King of Egypt, who was called Pharaoh, was worried. He saw that the Israelites were growing in number, and he was afraid that they would try to take over his land.

So Pharaoh made the Israelites into slaves and forced them to work for cruel Egyptian masters.

 Find the stickers to complete the picture.

A CRUEL LAW

Still the number of Israelites grew and grew, so Pharaoh made a cruel new law.

Pharaoh told his guards, "Every Israelite baby boy must be put to death!"

 Spot the five differences between the two pictures.

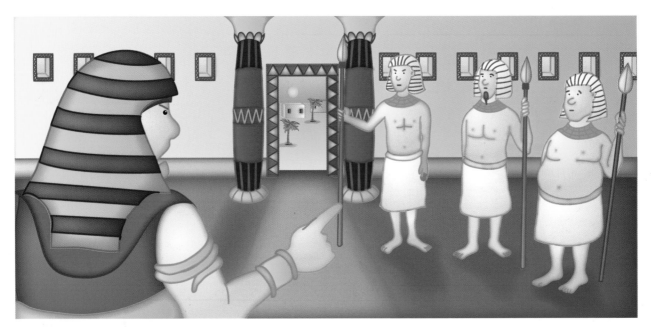

An Israelite woman named Yocheved had two children. Their names were Aaron and Miriam. When Yocheved heard about the law, she was very upset, because she was expecting a baby.

 Find the stickers to complete the picture. Now color it in.

HIDING THE BABY

Yocheved had her baby, and the whole family rejoiced. But they knew they would have to keep the baby hidden because it was a boy.

Aaron and Miriam kept watch at the windows. If they saw Pharaoh's soldiers nearby, they warned their mother. Yocheved always managed to find a safe place to hide the baby.

 Fill up the hiding places with the right stickers. Where has Yocheved hidden her baby?

THE BABY IN THE BULRUSHES

When the baby was three months old, he got too big to hide. So Yocheved made a plan.

She went to the river and gathered some bulrushes to make a basket, just big enough to hold the baby. Then she put her baby inside, wrapped up in a warm blanket. She and Miriam took the basket to the river, and hid it among the reeds.

"Stay here and watch your baby brother," Yocheved told Miriam. "Come and tell me what happens to him."

How many frogs can you find in this picture?
Can you find two that are exactly the same as each other?
Now find the stickers to complete the picture.

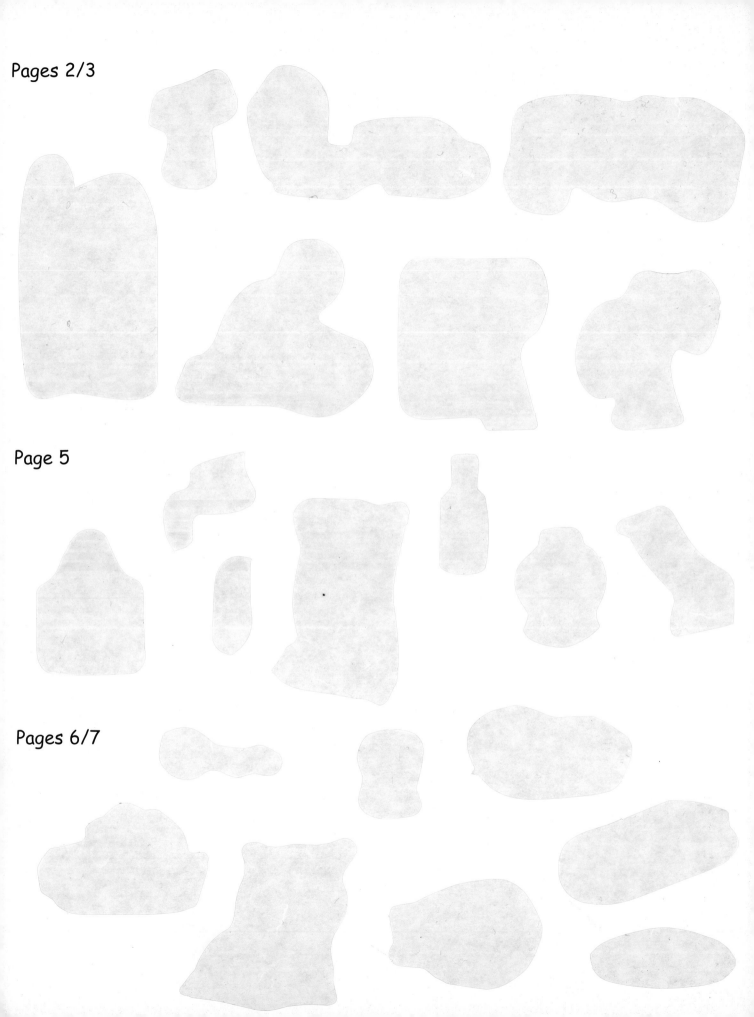

Pages 2/3

Page 5

Pages 6/7

ges 8/9

ges 10/11

ge 12

ges 14/15

PHARAOH'S DAUGHTER

Miriam hid in the tall grass near the river, and watched carefully.

In a little while, Pharaoh's daughter came down to the river to bathe. Miriam was very worried—what would happen if the baby was found?

As the princess waded into the river, she saw the basket in the reeds. "What can that be?" the princess wondered.

  Find the stickers to finish the picture.
Who will reach the basket?

MIRIAM'S IDEA

The princess looked inside the basket and saw a baby boy.

"This must be an Israelite baby!" she said. "He is so small and sweet—I won't let anyone harm him. I will take him back to the palace and raise him as my own."

When Miriam heard this, she had an idea. Coming out of her hiding place, she asked Pharaoh's daughter, "Shall I find an Israelite woman to be the baby's nurse?"

The princess said yes, and Miriam raced home to get her mother.

 Find five stickers to finish dressing the princess.

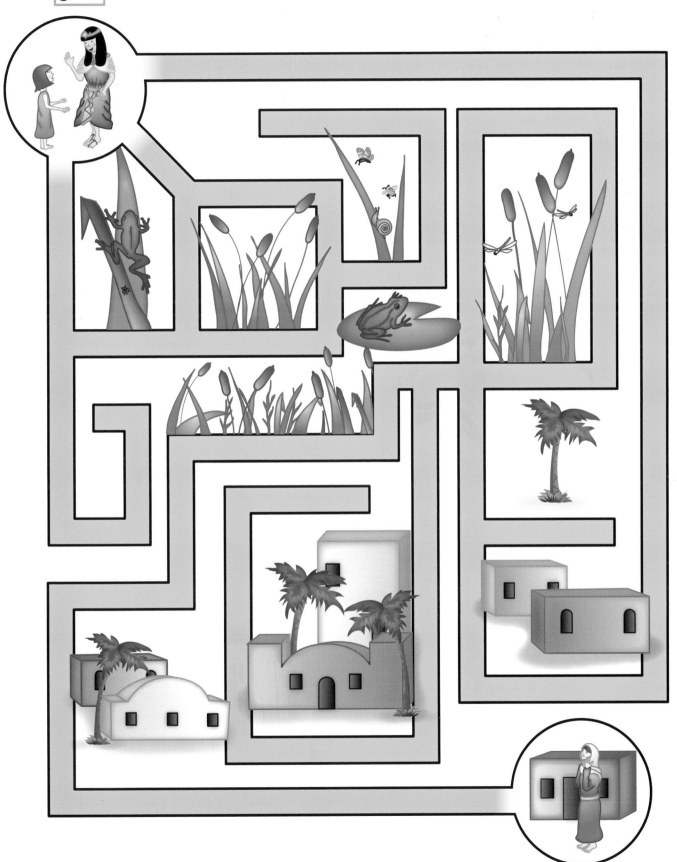

MOSES THE PRINCE

Pharaoh's daughter named the baby Moses, which means "draw out", because she drew him out of the water. And he was raised by his mother, Yocheved, in Pharaoh's palace.

Moses grew up as an Egyptian prince, but when he was old enough, his mother told him the story of his birth. So Moses knew that he was an Israelite, and that God had saved his life. When he was older, Moses became his people's greatest leader. He led the Israelites out of slavery in Egypt into the promised land of Israel.

 Find the stickers to complete the picture.
Now color in the scene of Pharaoh's palace.

ANSWERS

Page 4

Page 6/7

Yocheved has hidden her baby under the stool.

Pages 8/9

There are ten frogs in the picture.

Pages 10/11

The princess will find the basket.

Page 13